Small

A true story

About Attachment Disorder

That I sometimes wish

Was just a novel

EVA NAPIER

Second Edition

Village Lane Publishing

ISBN- 9781980255345

For Bonnie—
With Love from
Rebecca (Eva Napier)
+ Naomi (Ani).
Thank you for being real,
and for being a real friend.
♡

For all the children
suffering from Reactive Attachment Disorder,
and for the brave, exhausted, worn-down parents
who care for them-

May God bless you.

Eva Napier

CONTENTS

PREFACE

This is the true story of my journey adopting my 2-year-old daughter from Ukraine—and of my daughter Ani's journey as well.

Anastasia was born in Ukraine and given up by her birth mother on the day she was born. There was no room in the local orphanage, so for her first year of life, Ani was kept in a spare room at the hospital where they kept "extra" babies. They called this room the Baby Hospital. She was strapped down and not regularly held or spoken to for over a year. A bottle was propped up when she needed feeding. We were told that over ninety percent of the babies in the Baby Hospital died before they could be moved. Ani is a fighter. She lived.

When she was a year old, Ani was transferred to the local orphanage where she was given space to move, was held, and spoken to. She soon learned to crawl and walk, sit and talk. And she was still a fighter.

My now ex-husband and I arrived in Ukraine to adopt two children when Ani was two and a half years old. She was the tallest child in the room of approximately twenty-five two-year olds. Ukrainian law did not allow any information on available children to be sent out of the country, so we prepared our dossier and traveled there. We met with adoption officials in Kiev and told them we were hoping to adopt twins. They sent us to visit different orphanages as we searched for the children we felt were ours.

We found Ani and Sergey in the same orphanage—not biologically related, but both two years old. They had been living in the same small group since Ani arrived at the orphanage. Sergey had lived there since shortly after birth. Sergey cried when we held him and reached out for the orphanage mamas. I thought he would have a hard time adjusting to our home and family. Ani, on the other hand, seemed to warm to us immediately. She smiled and played with us, was clearly very bright, and was possibly the most charming child I had ever met. I was certain she would have no problem adjusting at all.

Heaven help my naïve soul.

It didn't take long to realize that while Sergey was an emotionally healthy little boy, something was very wrong with Ani. Our social worker had talked to us about the possibility, in Eastern European orphanages, of children developing Reactive Attachment Disorder, or RAD. The stories she told were horrifying, and I was confident I would recognize that any child with RAD was unwell, and would not adopt them. I was wrong.

Children with RAD come across as the most charming children on earth—as long as they do not feel threatened by love. What RAD kids fear most is attachment—a loving bond with another human being. Because of this, they learn to manipulate relationships to get what they need to survive— food, clothing and shelter—while keeping everyone at an emotional distance. When anyone threatens them with something as powerful as love, these kids react in ways guaranteed to push the threat away. Because mothers are often the most loving person in their lives, mothers are the ones they most often target for abuse. However, in order to make sure they still have access to food, clothing and shelter, RAD children will do everything they can to keep everyone else believing they are sweet and kind. They are master manipulators, even at exceptionally young ages.

I wrote this book because, after years of living with Ani, enduring her abuse and helping her overcome her fears of nearly everything, especially love, I realize that there is a gap in the literature on RAD children and their families.

Teachers, principals, social workers, therapists, friends and family members almost always underestimate the stress of living with a RAD child. Unless you have lived it, it is nearly impossible to fathom how intentional and manipulative RAD children can be. I yearned for a short book that could convey to the people we worked and interacted with some portion of what we were living at home.

This book is just that.

I hope that by sharing our story, other families with RAD children will have a resource to help them share their own story. I hope that professionals, friends and family members can begin to understand, in part, what the frazzled, dazed and beaten parents, especially mothers, are experiencing. And finally, I hope that other children like Ani will find the courage to open their hearts and experience the sweetness of love.

With all my heart,

Eva Napier

SMALL

Small
We found her
In the winter of Ukraine
Wearing a bow, too large for her head
And eyes
Blue as the frozen sky
Staring

She ate everything we brought
Grapes
Candy
Beef jerky
Wrappers

Her brother Sergey's food

Asking for more
   Smiling
Getting more
   Snuggling
Taking more
   Hitting the others away

A hungry girl

Paperwork
Lawyers
Paperwork
Translators
Paperwork
And long conversations
In a language
Of garbled sounds
My ears cannot untangle

The orphanage director
A large man
Watching us through pudgy eyes
Accused by post-communist bureaucrats
Of making it too easy
For parents
To bring orphan children home
His voice booms out
That he
Is an obedient citizen
And I almost laugh
Until I see his
Very
Serious
Eyes
And remember
This
Is no joke

A tiny office

In a crumbling building
Paint peels
From the clunking radiator
We perch on steel-cold chairs
A stern judge
Behind a wooden desk
Wets his stamp
With ink
Boom!
A red stamp
Boom!
A black stamp!
Boom!
Boom!
Boom!
He unwinds a red thread
Pulls a needle from his drawer
And sews the papers
Deftly
As if being a seamstress
Is part of his job
As if staplers
Have not yet been invented

And just like that
Anastasia and Sergey are ours

Leaving the orphanage
  Screaming
    Clinging
      Twisting
        Fighting
Tears course down her cheeks

As we wrestle her into a car seat
Straps and buckles
She pierces the air
Certain her life will end
Outside those cold gray walls

Dressed in new clothes
Kicking off her shoes
      I put them back on
Tearing off her coat
      I put it back on
Throwing her shoes
Tearing out her hair bow

I sit on the bed
Exhausted

Tears
And tears
  And screams
    And tears

McDonalds
Her first stop
In a new life
She clutches French fries
Refusing to eat
She glares
I dare you to look at me
Or talk to me
Or feed me
Or touch me

I wonder
Is something wrong?
But no
Just the shock
Of leaving
The only home
She has ever known

She'll be all right
With time

Sergey eats
And talks
And runs
And eats
And talks
Tiny Russian words
Tumbling out
As he pokes more French fries in

She falls asleep that night
In a dingy hotel room
One bare bulb on the ceiling
With French fries
Still clutched
In her tiny fists

An airplane
Over the ocean
Portioned food on plastic trays
She eats hers
  And mine

    And Sergey's

And the man across the aisle's
Her tiny fists reach out
Asking for more

Home
Home
Home!
For the first time ever
In their lives
Ani and Sergey are home!

And I cry
Relief
My older children--
All well
All hugging
All talking
All crying
Three weeks is too long
Too long to be apart

She hides
Behind my legs
Clings
Scowls

Come play! they say
Come smile!
Let me hold you!

No
No!
Nyit!

Something is wrong

Sergey smiles
Hugs
Talks
Plays
Russian jabber
And a smattering of
English words

Sergey plays
With a truck on the floor

"Beep, beep! Watch out! Coming through!"

I stop and stare
At his tiny face
Smiling up
Could that mean something
In Russian?
Or is it
English
Already?

But Ani
Is locked away

Her bedroom door
Bangs open
In the morning light
And she stands there
Feet apart
Glaring
At all the world

And I laugh
At one so small
And so fierce

She's only two

And daring
The world
To stop her

Fixing lunch
In the kitchen
I hear something
In the bathroom
She has Sergey
By the hair
Holding his head
In the toilet
Under water
I grab him
Hold him
Dry him
And look at her
She scowls
And looks away

Why…
Would she do that?

Books
On bonding
How to fall in love
With a child

That does not feel
Like my own

Prayers
For strength
For wisdom
Beyond my own

I wonder
Sometimes
When her mother will come
To the door
To thank me
For babysitting
And take her home

But she is mine
I know it
In my mind
Try to feel it
In my heart
I pray
Long hours
And read more
On attachment

Hold them
    Feed them
        Cuddle them
            Smile at them

She climbs
Onto my lap

And smiles
At me!
Relieved
I smile back
Her arms about my neck
She kisses me
Thrusting her tongue
Into my mouth
Her hands
Grope my pants
I spit
And shove her away
In complete disgust

Who is
This person
Disguised
As a toddler
And what is she doing
In my house?

A tiny hand
Reaching up
Pushing a button
Doors open
A neighbor man welcomes us
With a smile
Into the small box
Of the elevator
We step in
Ani smiles
Reaches for the man
He smiles back

And before I know
What she will do
She touches him
Holds him
In places
That leave only shock

On the man's once-smiling face

The doors open
And I am too stunned
To remember
Where we were going

We walk outside
To the car
Hurrying
With grocery lists
Library books
Errands
To do
But Sergey
And Ani
Stop
Stare
Up
Into the grey
And raining
Sky

What is it?
I ask
Only rain

Haven't you ever

Seen rain before?

And then I know
They have not
And suddenly
My list
Of things to do
Shrinks
To one
We smile
Into the dripping sky
Feeling
The wetness
Of rain
On our cheeks

More splashing
In the bathroom
Ani has Sergey
By the hair
Holding his head
In the toilet
Again
And again
And again

Winter melts
To southern spring
Cherry blossoms
Butterflies
Packing boxes bloom
All through the apartment

A new city
A new house
With a yard
Grass
Trees

Playing outside
A breeze
Brushes gently
And Ani screams
Throwing herself
At the lamp post
Clinging
Terrified
That she might
Blow away

Ani
Will Not
Step on the grass
On the sidewalk
On the wood floor
On the carpet
On any surface
Of any color
She has not tried
On anything
That might be different

The world is untrustworthy
Ready to swallow her up
Slip her into space
Or starve her

If given
Half a chance

A picnic in the park
She is eating
Everything
Children run
Playing
Rolling down the hill
Come!
Roll down the hill!
I lay her
On her back
But she is certain
She has been
Rolled into the sky
Lost in space
She clutches at the grass
And weeps
Gravity is not to trust
Food is not to trust
Mamas and Papas
Are not to trust
Only fear
Fighting
Survival
Clutching grass
Clutching french-fries
Clutching control
For fear of flying loose

She stands in the kitchen
And urinates on the floor

Smiling

And I
Am confused
She looks so pleased

As if she's done something
Very right

She smears a mess
Of her own feces
On the floor
On the walls
On my birthday
And when I come in
Throws them
In my face

At the park
She throws rocks
At me
Yelling my name

Practice sessions
With Sergey
On how to say no
To having his head
Held down
In the toilet

On the back deck
Sergey shrieks
Ani
Holds the insecticide

We use to kill spiders
Spraying Sergey
Head to toe
Telling him
To hold still
While he cries

What!
Are!
You!
Doing?!

I was only killing him
A little bit

I ask our doctor
What on earth
Is going on?
How can a child
Try to kill
Another child?

He just smiles
And tells me

It didn't happen

She didn't know
It was just a game
She didn't understand
What she was doing
Probably she thought
It was sunscreen

I think
Perhaps
It is the doctor

Who doesn't understand

But then again
Perhaps
I am crazy
Imagining such things

He must be right
I must be wrong
Perhaps I really am
Losing my mind

But
I do not let
Ani and Sergey
Play together
Anymore
Unless I
Am right there
In the room
Watching

I have become
A paranoid mother
My friends tell me
My husband tells me
I am too worried
About something
That is nothing

She's fine

Early Intervention
A chance
To give mom a break
For speech therapy
Occupational therapy
Physical therapy
Catching up
On all the things

They didn't do

In an orphanage
In Ukraine
But after a month
She is sent home early
One day
Another day
Every day
For different reasons
Never with a good explanation
She had a cold
She looked tired
She bonked her head
Sent away
From an exhausted teacher
To an exhausted mom
And I wonder
If the teacher sees
What I see
And how to ask
About a problem

I do not comprehend
At all

She has been peeing again
On the floor
Throwing food
On the floor
Making it look
Like an accident
But the small looks
She gives me
Just before she pees
Or drops saucy pasta
Or pours milk
Make me think
I must be crazy
She is only three

For Heaven's sake!

She is not capable
Of this sort
Of premeditation

I take her to the bathroom
Remind her
That we use the toilet
She leans back
Aims
And urinates
All over me

I gasp
She smiles

I grab her
Off the toilet
Yank her
Down the hall
Shove her
Twist her
Want to hurt her
Then stop

Stop

And cry

Crazy
This is crazy
She is crazy
I am crazy

I scoop her up
To hold her
But she screams
Grabs my hair
Yanks
Bites
Hits
Pinches
Twists

Don't!
Hold!
Me!
Ever!

I am her mother
I want to hold her
To love her
To tell her it will be ok
To spank her
To push her
Away
To never
Be her mother
Again

I sit
On the floor
Alone
With the phone book
Looking up
Numbers
There has to be someone
Surely there is someone
Who can help me
Help her
Or take her
Or me
Away

"Mommy, come with me!"
A big smile
She holds out her hand
And pulls me down the hall
To her bedroom
Her dresser
Gouged

Deep holes
How could this
Have happened?

She pulls
A knife
Large and sharp
From under her dresser
A butcher knife
From the kitchen

"This is what

I'll do to you

When you are asleep."

She smiles up at me
Sweetly
Holding
The knife

We rearrange bedrooms
She cannot sleep
In the same room
As her sister
An alarm
On her door
When she sleeps
Alone
At night
One that will scream
If she tries
To come out

I remember
A therapist
Before Ukraine
Talking
About crazy things
Telling me
Of a crazy disorder
Messed up children
Psychopaths
In tiny bodies
It was called
Attachment disorder

But no!

I know kids
I love kids
And that stuff
The things she told me
Were so unreal
It could never happen
To me
To my family
To my child
To my daughter
So pretty
Blond hair and blue eyes and lovely
And loved
It cannot be
It cannot be
I hope it cannot be
I wonder if it is

Another move
Across the country
More packing boxes
More moving men
More tears
She shoves me away

Don't hold me!

"Those men are angry with me."

Why do you think they are angry?

"Because
They took my bed apart
And they are taking

All my things."

She drinks water
  Asks for more
Drinks water
  Asks for more
Drinks water
  Asks for more
Vomits
  Asks for more
You cannot have
Any
More
Water

"But they are not packing the sink.
We will not have water

At our new house."
She asks for more

A new house
A new school
She says good-bye
On the first day
Without looking back
And the teacher smiles

"What a well-adjusted child!"

Leaving the store
Pockets full of candy

"I didn't take it."

Leaving the school
Backpack full of toys

"I didn't take them."

Sitting in a chair
Kicking the table

"I'm not kicking it."

"I don't hear any sound."

"You must be crazy."

And I think
I am

She takes Sergey
To the second story

Opens the window
Tells him to jump
With a shove on his back
And he is about to fall
When I run in
And close the window
And wonder
About all the parenting advice
I have ever received

What is the natural consequence
For homicide?

Comfy chairs
Dim lights
Soft questions
During intake
For therapy
Kind smiles
Until I explain
Why we are there

Phone calls
More offices
Sound machines
In the hall
Awkward pauses
Glances at Ani
Playing quietly
With a dismembered doll

No therapist
In the state

Will see her
Will treat her
Will even offer advice

She is beyond
The scope
Of my practice

You don't say

I think
She is well
Beyond the scope
Of my practice
As well

Ani
Smiles at dad
Scowls at mom
Kisses dad
Hits mom
Charms dad
Lies to dad
Tricks dad
Smirks at mom

Something is wrong
Very wrong
But dad says
She is a child
A small child
A pretty child
A lonely child

A child who needs
Our love

And mom knows
He is right
And she is right

Fighting
In the kitchen
In the bedroom
In the halls
Ani and mom
Ani and Sergey
Older kids
Mom and dad
Everyone

A note
From the school

"You did not send a lunch

To school with Ani today.
We bought her a hot lunch

Please send money."

I am confused
I thought
I packed
A lunch

But maybe not

The next day

I am careful to pack
A good lunch
And put it
In her backpack
But I get back
Another note

"Please send more money

And please remember
To pack her

A lunch."

I call the teachers
Tell them
Something is wrong
I did pack a lunch
She must have done
Something
With it

But to the teacher
Ani is sweet
  Kind
    Loving
      Charming
And would never
Do
Such a thing

The teacher
Has no idea
What Ani
Would

Ever
Do

I pack a lunch
And write a note
Telling the teacher
There is a lunch
In her bag
An apple
A sandwich
Crackers
And a drink
Please
Do Not
Buy her a hot lunch
Today

The phone rings

"Mrs. Napier

I am so confused
Your note says
You packed a lunch
But there is no lunch

In Ani's bag

And she says
You do not feed her dinner
Either
But lock her
In her room

During meals"

Silence

She said
That I do
What?

There is not even a lock
On her bedroom door
And she eats
Everything within reach
For every meal

How can I prove
My innocence

I pack
Another lunch
And write
Another note

In the morning
In her room
Blood
On her arms
On her clothes
On the walls

Washing
Arms
Clothes
Walls

You mustn't cut yourself

But she does
Again
And again
And again
Until
Almost
We do not notice
Blood
On arms
On clothes
On walls

Now normal
Looks like
Hitting
Sounds like
Screaming
Smells
Like urine
And is the color of
Blood

Alarms
On her bedroom door
To save us from
Knives in the night

Alarms
On the front door
To save her
From running away

Alarms

On the back door
To save pet rabbits
From slaughter

But not on her siblings' doors
And so a pet hamster
Is fed to the cat
A death toll
Of one
In what feels like
War

The fighting
Is almost more
Than I can bare

Dad says
You need to lighten up
Show her love
Be cheerful
She'll come around

I say
You need to crack down
Show her consequences
Be firm
She'll come around

The hate and fear
Have leaked
From her eyes
And heart

Into mine
Into his
Into the family
Slamming us all
Angry red
Fearful
And shivering
Into our own corners

Don't
hold
me

A phone call
Just to check
On divorce

It is possible?
Of course
It is possible

Therapy
For me
For him
For us

"Tell me,

What is wrong?"

I don't like him

We fight

I don't like her

We fight

"And what is the problem?"

Ani
Ani
Ani

"Ani?"

No, it is us
We fight

"About what?"

Ani
Ani
Ani

"I see."

In her room
She tears the eyes
From a stuffed tiger
Using the sharp backs
To cut her arms

We take them out
Stuffed rabbits
Dogs
And teddy bears
Piled in the basement
Out of harms way
Out of her way
And she cries
I want my teddy

Her blankie
Thrown
At the chandelier
In her room
Knocks off pieces
Of hanging glass
Angry cuts
Deep in her arms
Blood
Soaking
Everywhere

We take out the chandelier
And then look
At the bulb
Bare
Like a prison cell
Like an office in Ukraine
And know
It is not safe
Either
A room
With sunlight only

Is safer
Than broken glass

Before school
I step out of the kitchen
Only for a moment
To answer the door
Then back into the kitchen
And I stop
Staring
At drips of red
On the walls
On the counters
And on Ani
Sitting on the floor
Smiling

What did you do
Tell me
What did you do

She looks surprised
I didn't do
Anything

Sergey
Where is Sergey
Running
Calling
Sergey!
Sergey!

He is standing

In the bathroom
Washing his hands
With bubbly soap

No blood

No marks at all

And I think
I will faint
With relief

Then I find
Our dog
Our bleeding dog
And the fork
Red on the prongs
And I know
Sergey
  Could have been
    Bleeding
      Instead

More books
More research
Libraries
Bookstores
The Internet
Something
There must be something
Someone
Somewhere
Some treatment

For children
So hurt

Holding therapy
May be a way
To bring hope
To children
And families
Suffering with
Reactive Attachment Disorder
I read
And study
And pray
But it does not
  Feel
    Right

Am I crazy?
When there is something
That might help
Not to try?

But still
It does not
  Feel
    Right

I open her bedroom door
Ani stands
With one foot already out
Her third story window
A straight drop
To concrete below

Dad brings a hammer
And nails
Sealing the window
Against cool breezes
And leaps
To death

Ani screams
Throws herself against the wall
Grabs the hammer
And tears at her arms
With the pointed end
I tackle her
To the ground
She swings the hammer
Hitting me
On the head

I stop

She swings again
And I catch her arm
Wretch the hammer
From her grip
Her fingers tearing
At my skin
She shrieks
Ringing in my ears
Until my ears stop hearing
I pin her arms
Her teeth bite
My side pulls back

She bites again
I hold her head
Sit on her middle
Pin her arms again
And hold her
As she thrashes
Wild
Screaming

Until
She
Finally
Stills

I let her up
And she spits
In my face

In the news
A report
Of a family
Whose daughter died
Held
Too hard
Suffocated
Her bedroom
Stripped
Of all toys
Of furniture
Of lights
With locks
And alarms
On her doors

And a reporter
Noting how terrible
These parents are
To treat a child
Like this

I am still
Silent
Watching
Aching
With empathy

Martin Luther King Jr. day
At the dinner table
What did you talk about in school today?
A man was killed
Please pass the salt
Someone shot him
What do you think of the war in Iraq?
People are killed
Please chew with your mouth closed

I glance
At Ani
Locked in the highchair
That keeps her
From the table
From throwing food
And smashing glasses

But tonight
She has a necklace
Made of yarn

With a paper dove
A kindergarten project
To celebrate peace
On the day a man died
When the world is at war
She has twisted the yarn
Around her neck
Tight
And tighter
And tighter still
Her lips
Eyes
Cheeks
And face
Are all
Becoming blue

I leap
Across the room
And tear the yarn
From her fingers
From her neck
From her life
That remains
Tear Ani
From her chair

Still blue
She screams
And my ears
Are going deaf
From so much
Screaming

Why did you do this?

I just wanted
To die
A little
Bit

She does not
Ride the bus
To school
The next day

How can I talk to them about this?
About suicide
To the kindergarten teacher
My kindergarten
Child

At school
Teachers
Principal
Therapist
Suddenly listen
To me
Instead of
Ani
Suddenly scared
By the undeniable
Reality of

The "s" word

Suicide

"Is it possible
That there has been
Something traumatic

In her past?"

I only stare

Is it possible?
That you cannot know?
I have written letters
Have sat in meetings
Have called on the phone
Have tried so desperately
To tell you

And now you ask me
This?

Yes
Yes, it is possible
Yes, there has been
Something traumatic
In her past

Trauma

Is this child's life

A phone call
To a doctor
Across the state

Suicide
In a child so small
So young
So innocent

Innocent?

She is a candidate
For the state hospital
For the ward
For children
Who try suicide
Homicide
But at age five
She is still
Too young

Six to twelve
Are the ages we treat
She is still too young
Even for our youngest ward

"Talk to her
Reassure her
Life is well
Food is here
Care is here

Love is here"

But screaming
Screaming

Till my ears shut down
And register only
An angry
Rushing quiet
I cannot
Communicate
Anything

"Be firm

With consequences"

And what
Pray tell
Is the consequence
For suicide?

"Have rewards
And catch her
In good behavior"

And so I try
Desperately
To catch
A glimpse
Of good behavior
Between
The lies
The screams
The rudeness
And
All

The
Blood

"Thank you for eating so politely"

Her mouth
Begins hanging open
Food sliming out
Onto her shirt

"I like the way you're holding my hand as we shop"

Yank!
Her hand is gone
She turns
And runs
Out of the store
Into the street
Into the traffic
Not looking back

"You got on your pajamas! That's great!"

Her hand
Unbuttons
The top
Letting her pajama shirt
Fall to the floor
As she stares
Right
Into
My

Eyes

I dare you
To compliment me
Again

My other children
Have no mother
I am only
The prison guard
Keeping Ani alive
Keeping us alive
Trying to keep
Some small bit
Of sanity
Alive

Talking
To my other children
I never see you
I never talk to you
When we are home
Ani is home
Could we try
Homeschool
A break
During the day
While Ani is at school
For the rest of us
To be
Together?

Books

Lessons
Warm sunlight
At the kitchen table
Conversations
That can be heard
Without screaming
A moment
Of sanity
In the center
Of every day

Therapy again
For mom and dad

"What do you think
Is the root cause
Of your problems?"

Maybe this
Maybe that

"Maybe Ani?"

Silence

"I've given much thought
To this situation
And I've come
To a very tough decision"

Silence

"Either you
Will find a way
To remove Ani
From your home

Or I
Will be forced to file
Reports
Of child abuse
Not for Ani
But to protect
Your other children
It is not fair
To make them

Live with her"

From the empty pit
Of my heart
Where feelings used to live
Something rises
And breaks through
In the form
Of a sob

I cry
And cry
And cry
And cry

Until I can

Almost
Stop

"Why are you crying?"

I don't know
But I think
I am relieved

But
I love her
We cannot do this
She is our child
We have a responsibility
We must care for her
I will care for her
To the end

"At the expense of your marriage?

And your other children?"

Silence

Is that the cost?

"It is the cost."

Then she can go

In September
Ani will turn six

In September
On her birthday
Ani will enter
The state hospital

We tell her the news
Expecting screams
Her only form of communication
Except for lies
But we are met
With an indifferent
Shrug
And a faint hint
Of her relief

For two weeks
We do laundry
Pack bags
Shop for towels
And bedding
And it almost feels
Like summer camp

A photo album
With pictures
That lie
About a happy family
Without tears
Much more quiet
Than real life

And through it all
Ani

Is almost
Happy
And the house
Is strangely
Calm

We open presents
A few days early
And pretend

It isn't so

A blanket!
A bathrobe!
A photo album!

And with a smile
That almost looks real
She thanks us all

Happy Birthday, Dear Ani
Happy Birthday to you

Suitcases
Packed
  And I am
    Almost
      Sad
        To see her go

SMALL

She picks up her bag
And follows dad
Out the door
To the plane
Across the state
Without looking back
Without a hug
Without a single
Good-bye

I love you!
I call

She does not
Turn around

I go to my room
And cry
For the loss
Of what could have been
With relief
For what may yet be
And with confusion
About what is

A cloud
Has passed
From our house

Sunshine
Might be visible
Although we almost

Do not know
What it is

Dad comes back
A torn and empty
Soul

How can you be happy?
Why do you all smile?
Be sad!
Be sad, he says
Ani is gone! We miss her
Says dad

We do not talk
When Dad is here
We are solemn
And grave

But he knows
We are happy
And he is angry
With our happiness
And we are sad
With his anger
And we are quiet
With the sudden return
Of sanity

Her room
Is repainted
Blue and green
To cover the blood

So hard to
Wash away

And a strange thing
That might be peace
Settles like a nervous bird
On the windowsill
Of the house

School for the children
Work for Dad
And phone calls
During phone call time
To Ani

I am fine
I love it here
This place is the best
When can I come home?
This hospital stinks
I hate it here
Crying

A long trip
Visits
To family therapy
At the hospital

"Mom
You and Ani

Will play in this room
While the doctors watch

Through the mirror."

She smiles
And takes me into the room
To show me the doll house
The little kitchen
I like your picture
Yes, please!
More juice
She picks up a doll
And laughs
As she throws it
Right at my face
Then another
Then wooden blocks
And plastic dishes

I am bruised
Inside and out
When I leave the room
And the doctors say
That went well
She was able to express her feelings
Toward you

Back at home
Dad says
We'll be settled in by New Years

What?

What are you talking about?

You aren't making any sense

Oh
Did I forget to tell you?
I got a new job

What?
What are you saying?
You got a new job?

You didn't tell me this!
Where?

Closer to Ani

SO!
So, we are all moving!
And you forgot to mention this!
You got a new job?
I cannot believe
You got a new job

And you didn't ask

You didn't talk to me

You only say-
Did I forget to mention
That I got a new job?

The frightened bird
That was almost peace
Is gone
In the downpour

Of bitter rain

Packing boxes
Again

A new house
Much smaller
A square box
Built with no imagination
Crammed full
Of family
Worries
Children
And boxes

Are there enough bedrooms?
Where will I sleep?

Why don't the dishes
Fit in the cupboard?
Why do we all
Have to sleep
In the same room?

Where will Ani sleep
When she comes home?

Will she come home?

New schools
New questions
How many children do you have?
I only want to answer
Never Mind

Friends
Neighbors
Church
And life begins
To look
Like normal

The phone rings
Ani
The doctors tell me
Has the psychological profile
As a serial killer

I remember to breathe
And wonder
How a mother responds
To that

We are trying a new approach
They say
With material
From the state prison
And new medications
To help her

I nod
Wet my lips
And ask them to
Let me know
How it goes

We rake leaves in the yard
Go sledding
Plant flowers
And watch the leaves turn green
And yellow again

A phone call
One night
Saying Ani is ready
After fifteen months
Of treatment
To come back home

No

She can't be

I know she's not ready
Not yet
Please

See my heart
It is still scarred
Scratched
Raw
And not ready
Not yet
Please

The date is set
Pushed back
Set again
Set for sure
Not to be changed

Ani
Is coming
Home

Is she better?

Dreaming
I drive the car
At night
Afraid
Because there is a murderer
In the back seat
Hiding
Thinking I do not know
He is there
I look
In the mirror
Into the backseat
And see a head
Rise
And I scream
At the sight
Of blond pig-tails
I wake
Sweating

We move the children
To different bedrooms
So Ani can have a whole room
To herself

It's too cramped

I can't move
Where will my clothes fit?
Why does she get her own room?

Do you want to share a room
With Ani?

No

Well, then
Make do

Meetings at school
We have a daughter
Coming home
After fifteen months
In the state hospital

She clears her throat
He looks at his pen
Someone asks
Fifteen months?
Another asks
What did she do?
Why is she there?

And because I am scared
I tell too much
Of the truth
Fear leaking from me

Into them

A special school
For handicapped children
Near our hospital
So she can be safe
It will be just the place
They all assure me

But I know
It is not Ani
Who needs to be kept safe

Can I visit the school?

Oh no
No
Not now
Sign the papers first
Then you can visit
All you want
But first
Sign the paper
Saying she will attend
The special school
And they all
Look at me
Like dogs
With a rabbit
In close pursuit
And I am suspicious
Because something
Is not right

I look for the school
Online
And find that it is
For special children
But not for children
Like Ani

These children
Are severely retarded
They do not read
Or learn
Or eat
Or sit
On their own

This is not Ani

She has many problems
But Ani
Is also
Very smart

I call the school
And tell them
They have not understood
What Ani needs
Or how she works
Or who she is
You have no choice
They say
To sign
Or not

This is the only school
She may attend
And if you do not sign
She will have to be home schooled
We cannot offer
Any
Other
Choice
So let us ask again,
Will you sign?

I pause
Before I answer
Let me think
Just let me think

A phone call
To the school district
To the office for children
With special needs
I explain
That Ani may have problems
With behavior
But she is still
Very
Very
Bright

She loves math
She loves good jokes
She can throw a football
With a perfect spiral

And hit a baseball
Far outfield
She needs to be challenged at school
Or she will spend her time
Planning
Ways

To…
Well
Never mind

Mrs. Napier
Let me explain
Our responsibility
To your daughter

We do not need
To provide
An education
To anyone
We only need
To provide
An environment
Where a child could learn

If your daughter
Can read Dick and Jane
Today
And if she
Can read Dick, Jane and Spot
Next year
We have done our job

Silence

On my end
Of the phone

Can you repeat that?
I'd like to write down
What you just said

You bet!
If your daughter
Can read Dick and Jane
Today
And if she
Can read Dick, Jane and Spot
Next year
We have done our job
Got it?

It's not our job
To teach your daughter
Anything

Well
I think we now
Understand each other
Thank you for your time

Several letters
On the computer
In the mail
Phone calls
To everyone
I can think of
Who might know something

About Special Education Laws

Principal
School board
State legislator
Congressman
Senator
Advocacy groups
And Lawyers

The phone rings
It is the principal
The same principal
Who had said
There was no other option

But today
She sounds
Almost nervous

Please, tell me
Mrs. Napier
What we can do for you
What do you want?
How can we help you?
You tell us
How school will be
For Ani

I am stunned
Into silence

Can we meet
Soon
To discuss
What you would like?

Yes
Of course
We can meet

Back at school
In the same room
With the same people
But the same papers
Are somehow missing

Ani needs
A small classroom
I say
With only a few children
And a few teachers
Who know how to work with children
With emotional disabilities

Yes
We can do that
No problem
Of course

I sign
New papers
Almost not believing
The change

November wind blows chill
And my thoughts
Dart back to an orphanage
In Ukraine
As I wait for her
In the airport

Taller
A different haircut
And blue eyes
Unsure
Darting from here
To there

All the kids
In the car
Squeezing in
Making room
For one more
Returned

As we round the bend
And see the house
A chorus of young voices

We're home!

Ani asks
Do they always say that?

In her room
A mattress
A blanket
A stuffed tiger
And a girl

Small
In an empty room

With an alarm
On the door

Good night
Good night
Good night

I lay awake
And listen
And wonder
And listen more
What have we done?

What have I done?

The teacher
Is new
Just out of college

Good morning Ani!

A small class
Two teachers
No privileges
Until she earns them
And a tiny corner
Of myself
Thinks
Maybe
Things

Will be
All right
At school

At home
Playdough
Smashed into the cracks
Of the wood floor
Rubbed into the carpet
Ground into the curtains

"What Playdough?

I didn't touch any Playdough."

The toenail
Of her big toe
Is peeled back
And bleeding
She smiles

A band-aid
And she is back to play

Blood on the carpet
Spots of red
And of panic

"I don't know how

The band-aid came off."

The toenail

Is now
Completely
Gone.

Come
Play in this room
Where I can see you
But when I turn
To pour noodles
Into boiling water
She is gone

Ani?

Ani?

I look
In the front room
In the entry way
In the bathroom

Ani?
Where are you?
Answer me!

Down the stairs
She skips
Looking surprised

"I just went

To get my crayons"

On the wall
At the top of the stairs
Are long lines
Of blue
And green
And orange

You will sit
On this chair
And not get off
Again

Screaming
She throws herself
Off the chair
Onto the floor

"Why can't I color?

Why can't I play?
You never let me
Have any fun

At all!"

The noodles have boiled over
Spilling slimy water
On the hot stove
I pull the pan
Off the burner
And see Ani
Peeling another toenail

I kneel long
In prayers that night

In silence
Pondering
My role
Pleading
For help

A woman
At church
Standing beside spring flowers
Asks
Would Ani like to come

To my daughter's
Birthday party?

I stare
In shock
At such a thought
And say only that

I don't think
That would be
A good idea

The woman laughs
Lighten up!

She's eight years old!

Let her have fun
Children need friends
And freedom

I can't reply
There is no answer

For such a rational
Insane
Idea
At the top of the stairs
Ani pushes Sergey
And he falls
Screaming
Bangs his head
As I pray
Unrealistic
Hopeful prayers
That this was just
An accident

She screams
Hits me
Bangs her head
And throws herself
Across the room

I am no good!
Ani screams
No good for anyone!
Even after
The hospital
I am still trying
To kill people!

I abandon my prayers
In shock
That she is feeling
So upset
About hurting him

I will never be better!
I am too bad!

She cries
Real tears
And tells me
At eight years old
That life
Is too long
And too hard
To keep living

And with surprise
I realize
I might
Love
Her

Outside the store
In the sweltering summer
I empty her pockets
Again
And we go back in
Again
To return
A spool of thread
And three small bells
To the manager
Trinkets
She did not need
But stole anyway

I go to the library
To look for books
To search for books
To plead for books
Without finding
Any books
On parenting a child
With kleptomania

In the autumn chill
Outside a store
She lifts the legs of her jeans
Exposing her ankles
To biting wind

"Check my socks, too, Mom

That's where
Sometimes
I hide things
So you won't find them."

I look up
Surprised
At the honesty
Of that confession

Screaming
Hitting
Stronger than she was before

I push her
Into her room
Hold the door

As it shakes
With pounded rage
Crashes
With thrown furniture
She actually threw
A couch
Across the room
Will someone
Please
Call nine, one, one

The hospital
In this city
Will only take children
For one week
Until they are stable

What if she is not?

She will be

Arts
Crafts
And lots of TV
She is happy
For a vacation
From people
Who dare to love her

We pause
Almost catching
Our breath
And brace ourselves

For her return

A therapist
Would be good

Of course!
We work
With the most
Disturbed children

Sitting on a leather chair
In a large office
With dim lights
Her file is open
On the table before us

The doctor's eyes scan the page
Reading our reality
For the first time

A pause
As she considers
What she had not known

This is not
My area of expertise

Do you know
Another doctor?
Can you recommend
Someone else?
Anyone?

We have already called them
We talked to her
He is not available

They won't see her
Perhaps group therapy?

Of course!
We often have
Difficult cases
It will not be a problem

Another office
A leather chair
Dim lights

Her file is open
On the table between us

We must be careful
Mrs. Napier
Not to expose
Our other patients
To a dangerous child

I'm so sorry

We cannot help you
Here is your bill

The library
The internet
Books
Research

What has been done
What can be done
What can we do
Ourselves
Without a degree
But enough hours
To travel from here to the moon
And back again
I become

The world's leading authority

On kleptomania
Suicide
Violence
Homicide
Attachment Disorder
And Ani

With calloused knees
Tear stained cheeks
And prescriptions
For serious
Psychiatric medications
From the one doctor
Who will see Ani
But who also

Has Alzheimer's

And does not remember
Anything
About her history
From one appointment
To the next
I come up

With what almost looks
Like a plan

The things in this box
Cost fifty points
A lamp in your room
Costs two hundred points

You did your homework
At the table
Without yelling
You may have
Five points

She walks
Across the room
To mark her points
And I see the scratch
On her arm
Angry
Red
But not quite bleeding
And I tell her
Hurting herself
Means all her points
Are gone

I don't care!

I don't want stupid points!
And she scratches her arm
Harder

A good night
Turns into
Screaming
As the other children
Creep to their rooms
Abandoning hope
Of love
Or attention
Or even thoughts
From Mom

Closing her door
Turning on her alarm
A small voice says

Good night, Mom

I pause

Open the door

Good night to you, too
Ani

The end of a school year
Her second school year
Home from the hospital
I sit
In the classroom
Going over
What they call

Ani's progress
But what looks to me

Like lack of progress

She scored 100%
On all her reading comprehension tests

But how is that possible?
She does not understand
Anything
She reads
At home

"We make sure

All our students

Succeed!"

The teacher explains

"I stand behind her chair

While she takes her tests
And if she is about to mark
An answer that does not look
Right
I suggest
She may want
To try another

In this way
All our children

Succeed!"

I can see
That we do not see
Eye to eye

On education

I discover
From Ani
That there have been
Bus rides
With little boys
Too happy
To touch places
They should not
When those places
Are offered

I look at
Options
All options
A new school
A private school
A boarding school
But only one option
Looks like it might
Work

And I don't like it

I try to find another way
I try to find
Something
Anything
That is not
Homeschool

But while I am driving

Silent
Thinking
Considering options
Hoping homeschool
Is not
The only way
Ani says
From the backseat
I want to be home with you
To be homeschooled
Like the other kids

I am shocked
And as surprised
As I have ever been
At anything
She has ever done

Really?
Why?

Because
You do things together
You have fun
You are all friends
And I am not

I want to be your friend
Too

I order books
Reading
Writing

And Insanity

What have I done?
What will I do?

Autumn leaves
Red
Dripping
Like blood
And I realize
She has not
Cut herself
For quite a while

She pulls out books
Happy to play school
I check her answers
A few red checkmarks
And she is screaming
Again

I did not do it wrong!
I am right!

But she fixes
The mistakes
And after
One hundred
And twenty-nine
Next times
She screams
A little less

Reading
Is
Horrible
Pain
Torture

Don't make me do it!

I won't!

After she finally reads
One short story
I ask
What does it mean?

  I don't know
What did they say?

  I don't know
Why did they do that?

No answer

We put away the books
That are supposed to be
On her level

We get out
Picture books
Simple
Easy for a girl of ten
Tall for her age
Frog and Toad
And Dr Seuss

What does it mean?

 I don't know

  But maybe…

    Does it mean this?

A story
In a magazine
About a boy
Who stole a toy train
And felt bad

"He felt bad

Because he didn't want

To get caught"

No
That is not why

"Then why?"

You tell me

"I don't know"

When he gave it back
How did he feel?

"I don't know"

Then read it again

"I still don't know"

He felt better
Because he knew
He was doing what was right

She stares
Her eyes
An open picture
Of confusion

"How could someone feel better
If they give back
The thing they stole?"

Days in the park
Where all the children
Play tag
And space pilot
And explorers

Except Ani

She is alone
On a swing
As far
From the others
As she can get
But sometimes
For a moment

I catch her
Watching

We leave the store
And she holds out her arms
She knows the drill
I frisk her

Pause

And frisk her again

Nothing there

I look at her eyes
Blue, staring

Did you take anything?

No

I walk to the car
And drive home
In silence

"My math is done
Can I write a letter
To grandma?"

Why?

"I miss her"

I consider
The possibilities
What could she do
What could she gain
What is her reason
Hidden
For writing to Grandma?

I can find nothing

She has a pencil
And a paper
And writes the words
I love you grandma

I almost cannot bring myself
To mail those words away
I wish they were
For me

Another Christmas
And we wait
For thrown couches
The hospital number
Close by

But Ani watches everyone
Open presents
And bounces with excitement
When it is her turn
To choose a present
From beneath the tree

In afternoon sunlight
She takes her new treasures
To her room
Turns on the lamp
That she earned
With two hundred points

She has a book of stories
About Ramona and her mother
A new doll
Which is allowed
Because her old one
Has survived
For almost a year
With her throat intact
Though her hair is shorter
And colored pink
With a permanent marker

Her reading comprehension
Has improved
So quickly
I am thrilled
At the excellence
Of my own teaching

Checking her answers
I find whole sentences
With real ideas
Where only a word
Incomprehensible
Would have been scribbled before

But
Wait
Does she even know
A word like this?

At the back of the book
I find the place
With all the answers
Word for word
Exactly as she
Has copied them
And I make her
Do it all

Again

Screaming
Throwing pencils
But after
Only a few days
Of refusing
To write
She begins to work
Again

It is clear to me
Her only thought
Is on survival
If the answers are there
Why would I not copy them?

Footsteps

Nearly silent
Coming downstairs
One evening

"Will you take these

Needles and thread?
I had them in my room
But I kept poking
And poking
And poking
My finger

And I don't want

To start

To do it on purpose."

Her fingertip
Red
Pin pricks of blood

What are you making
With the needles and thread?

A quilt
She says

I'm making a quilt
From different scraps
Of fabric
That Grandma gave me
All the colors
Sewn in a crazy way
Look at how I put them together
Like this

Her eyes
Sincere
Her hands
Holding out
Weapons
Surrendered

And bits of fabric
Raw edges
Held with uneven stitches
Sewn in a way
That makes no sense
But all the same
Is strangely beautiful

A crazy quilt

And I dare to believe
That these may be
The shapes
And colors
Of recovery

THE MAGIC LOVE SONG
BY ANI NAPIER

An original story written by Ani when she was eight years old, about a year after she came home from the state psychiatric hospital.

While it is, of course, fiction, it shows much of how she saw her life at this time.

The word choices are all her own.

Once a pawn a time there was a beautiful kingdom named Gondola. It was a huge kingdom with a lot of wild deer, fish, bears, and jackrabbits and a huge meadow of wildflowers, berries and tree blossoms.

One day there was a beautiful princess with hair as golden as the afternoon sun that warmed the afternoon breeze and eyes as blue as the midday sky. She was running around in the meadow picking wild flowers making the most beautiful bouquets in the world when she bumped into an old man who in the story is a wicked wizard.

"Oh! Pardon me!" said the princess as she looked him in the eyes.

"Oh that's all right," the old man croaked.

The princess loved to make friends so she gave the old man the flowers and began to plod down the road to the palace when the old man stopped her and croaked, "I must give you a gift too." So he gave the princess a rose to take home.

The princess skipped happily down the road and into her room where she stopped to smell it. Ohh! Wait! I forgot to tell you that the flowers had a spell on them that when you smelled them you would be so grumpy that no one would know what to do. And the only thing that would break the spell is a Love Song. And BANG she turned into the grumpiest person in the world.

Now the queen and king just did not know why the princess was acting like this. So they kept her in her room so that she would not hurt anyone.

Days passed by when the prince came to see the princess. The queen and king did not like him but they so wanted their girl to be normal. So they told the prince that if he could get her acting normal then he could marry her if he kept good care of her.

He said he would and he went upstairs to her room and sang in his sweet voice a love song which was her favorite song.

She was so surprised that she turned around and threw a rotten tomato at him before she recognized the song and SNAP the spell broke. And that is when they fell in love.

So they lived happily ever after. But of the wizard, all I know is that he did not live happily ever after.

THE END

EVA NAPIER

ABOUT THE AUTHOR

Eva Napier is an author, entrepreneur, wife to the most amazing man on earth, and mother to six incredible children. She grew up in Minnesota, graduated from high school in Morocco, and has since lived in Saudi Arabia, South Korea, the Netherlands, and several places across the United States. Eva has an MA in International Business and Policy from Georgetown University. She is a serial problem solver who is dedicated to making the world a better place by helping individuals reach their full potential. When not writing, launching a business, or life coaching, she can be found reading superhero novels and sipping herbal tea in front of the fire.

96892105R00069

Made in the USA
Columbia, SC
04 June 2018